PEMBROKESHIRE'S HIDDEN HAVEN

Published by Celtic Maritime Connections with the support of the West Wales Maritime Heritage Society, Milford Haven Port Authority and South Hook LNG.

Milford Haven Port Authority

ISBN : 978-0-9560490-0-1

*Excerpts from "Down the Slipway" by David James. **Text provided by Keith Johnson (Pembrokeshire Life).

Aims of the West Wales Maritime Heritage Society include their presence at community events to help broaden the knowledge of maritime culture in West Wales.
Celtic Maritime Connections is a Europe Interreg III funded project.

Designed by Signum 1226 Ltd, Haverfordwest 01437 781333 www.signummedia.co.uk

Milford Haven

Exploring
Pembrokeshire's Hidden Haven

Contents

REFLECTIONS

There is nothing so evocative as a great waterway.

It is along this waterway that the blue-stones from the Preseli Mountains were rowed on their incredible passage to Stonehenge, or so we must believe if we are to account logically for their otherwise mysterious presence in the Wiltshire countryside.

Here also with a French fleet landed Henry Tudor to join forces with his Welsh compatriots and march upon the English throne. With what excitement and colour must that landing have been greeted; and think of the look-out who, upon St Ann's Head sighted first their sails and foreign flags, and knowing that some great enterprise was afoot ran breathless to take the news of this arrival to the waiting forces ashore and flash a signal from Benton to Carew to light the beacons.

Here too lay Nelson's fleet at anchor, the great ships of the line swinging on the tide, ship-shape and Bristol fashion, their topsides and spars glinting in the sunlight. The huge crews working in the rigging, preparing the sails, carrying water and provisions, cannon balls and barrels of powder, the ship's bells striking the half hours, watches changing on deck, boats coming and going, and perhaps the Admiral himself the centre of a magnificent cortege, setting off in his barge up river for a dinner party at Slebech Hall. Looking up at one of these great ships you would see a mass of gilded carving, foliage, wreaths, cherubs, heraldic symbols and ropework, all festooned about the windows of the stern, with lanterns and balconies and galleries, a dazzling tour de force of the wood carvers art. Rowing up towards the bow the lines of sombre gun ports row upon row, would greet your eye, those that could give forth the terrible English broadside, and when ready to make sail, hearing sailors shortening in the cables to the capstan shanty.

Consider too Brunel, with his dream of a great passenger terminal at Neyland for Ireland, possibly America, and employing for this purpose his revolutionary new ships, the Great Western and the Great Eastern. The latter becoming famous for laying the transatlantic telegraph cable.

I dare you to stand for a while alone at Picton Point on a howling winter's night and watch the clouds flying past the moon. Here came the ferry from Landshipping, for hundreds of years the regular and shortest route across the river Cleddau. Sailors returning to their ships, farmers with sheep and cattle swimming, merchants and tradesmen with their wares, pilgrims on their way to St David's, and crusaders returning from the Holy Land - all would have crossed here, and Cromwell's army en route to destroy Haverfordwest? At no time would you have been alone here then; but now just the mud, and the tide bringing down clumps of weed, the eerie cry of night flighting birds, the wind howling and the clouds.
Are you sure that you are still alone?

It is fascinating to imagine such scenes and the events which surrounded them in their same settings today. There seem to be few places so apt as the Haven for reflections and speculations of this kind, places where the past mingles with the present as if frozen in time.

The Haven, sphinx-like, will guard its secrets. "It flows along forever with trees on either hand" and this Secret Waterway will reveal to you much or little, as you may allow it, or as it judges you fit to receive.

Sir David Mansel-Lewis
President of West Wales Maritime Heritage Society

Those of us who are lucky enough to live or work on the waterway are well aware of its beauty and fascination so wonderfully displayed in this book.

Indeed so rewarding can be the experience that a certain degree of possessiveness can enter into the way in which we seek to describe it to those who have not yet had the advantage of experiencing the pleasures it can give. Perhaps then the title "The Hidden Haven" reflects not only the unknown nature of the area particularly in its upper reaches but also a tendency to keeps its delights to ourselves so as to preserve many of the aspects which provide it with such value.

However this runs alongside a great pride in what we all contribute to making this waterway so special and the genuine willingness to demonstrate and show that off to as wide an audience as possible.

That is what makes this publication so special, in that all who read it cannot fail to be impressed with the history, scenery, geography and activity in this wonderful waterway. Please do read it, enjoy it and come visit it for yourself and share our pride in being part of this gem.

Ted Sangster
Chief Executive
Milford Haven Port Authority

Ted Sangster

THE LOWER HAVEN

THE LOWER HAVEN

St Ann's Head

Approaching the Haven, St Ann's Head lighthouse stands resolute on the north-western shore of Pembrokeshire. To commercial seafarers and yachtsmen alike this marks the entrance to a haven of hidden gems; the white paint glimmers in the sunshine, or its bright light circling the night-time horizon in its own familiar identifiable pattern, or the eerie fog-horn echoing to sailors in the gloom. It seems apt that such a remarkable lighthouse should also keep watch over the haven, protecting the secrets that lie beyond its reach. Its guiding sights and sounds have offered safety to many thousands of mariners wary of the dangers lying off St. Ann's Head and the Pembrokeshire coastline.

"To visit St Ann's Head on a clear day when the blue waters of the bay meet the white foam of the crashing waves below and see the horizon..."

The waterway once bustled with various sailing vessels, passing between Skomer and heading around the mainland. From Viking ships to flying-boats, coastal fishing craft and traders to ferries, warships and tankers, this is just a short list of the plethora of which have berthed here. During the 18th and 19th Century many ships were built along the haven within the safety of its creeks and pills.

The Lighthouse

Going back to the 15th Century a light has stood here marking the headland, from the first decaying windmill like tower reported by George Owen, a traveller and diarist in the 1590s to today's gleaming white high technology, one can only wonder at the history that has passed before it. Like a Cyclops looking down, seeing Henry Tudor, the men, the warriors, the trade, the ships that it has guided safely into this wonderful haven turning the pages of history under its watchful eye.

St Ann's Light

The Lighthouse in 1920

Mill Bay & the landing of Henry Tudor

The shore of Mill Bay is nestled within the lee of the eastern side of St Ann's Head, known for its ample shelter from prevailing westerlies. Henry Tudor famously landed here from France with his fleet on 7th August 1485 and marched onwards, rallying support as he travelled towards Leicestershire where the Battle of Bosworth Field was won and he became king of England.

Defences

Before the 16th Century, defence in the peninsula of South West Wales utilised castles and encampments sited against land-based attacks. Sir Thomas Cromwell was one of the first in power to acknowledge the need for sea defences. In 1539 this led to the emergence of a general scheme in which King Henry VIII was most likely consulted. Forty-one years later work commenced on the West and East Blockhouses, at opposing sides of the entrance to the Haven and its Waterway. This was the only section of the plan to be completed. The continued fear of invasion made the need to protect the shipyards on the Waterway a priority. This was enough to generate further planning activity though little was realised. Only rarely were any more structures built. Pill Fort, an armed encampment and gun emplacement was constructed in 1643 by Royalist forces, and attacked soon afterwards by Parliamentarians. Situated to the east of where Milford now stands the battle involved both military and naval forces. Further defensive schemes were ordered by the Privy Council in 1689 but, as with those of 1748, nothing materialised. Belatedly, following a further review in

Henry VII
©englishhistory.net

Dale aerial view

the late 1840s a gun tower was erected at Stack Rock, a battery on Thorn Island, a fort at Dale Point and second fort at West Blockhouse.

Port of Dale

During the 16th and 17th centuries the Ports of Dale and Angle were amongst the busiest trading ports on the coast; sitting opposite each other at the entrance to the Haven.

A vast coastal path arches its way around Marloes Sands and covers a variety of scenery from rough rocky

Dale

Stack Fort

shorelines to wooded creeks and tidal mudflats. It is the only National Park in the UK which stretches for 187 miles around the coastal region of Pembrokeshire and provides a glimpse to the beauty of the county from the coast.

Remains of the main runways of the Second World War airfield at Dale can still be seen, though its quiet landscape belies the intense action that once threatened the land around it. Flight is more peaceful nowadays. Many thousands of sea birds nest on the nearby islands of Gateholm, Skokholm and Skomer, with Gannets favouring the more distant Grassholm, the largest colony in north-west Europe.

Sandy Haven

Marloes Sands

Ale

Ale brewed in the village of Dale by the Runwae family was in such demand that it was traded as far away as Bristol and Liverpool. Dale men owned a number of small trading smacks for this purpose. During the 18th Century this prosperous trade declined and by 1748 the jetty had fallen into disrepair. This determined the fate of the village which, became more and more deserted, and was in a ruinous state by 1801. Nevertheless a small stalwart population of fishermen and shipwrights persisted, managing to keep Dale alive throughout the 19th Century.

The Mary and May

Sailing Coasters

Captain Henry Beer was a descendent of Pembrokeshire's last seafaring family. From his base at Sandy Haven his small fleet of sailing coasters traded along the English and Welsh coasts to Newport, Gwent, ports in north Cornwall and to Liverpool.

Sandy Haven

As we sail east from Great Castle Head towards South Hook Point we pass three smaller bays whose names conjure up images of tales and lore; Longoar, Butts and Sleeping Bays, names we can only wonder of their origin, leading us to the inlet of Sandy Haven.

In Pembrokeshire inlets such as Sandy Haven are described as a creek or a pill, as is typical, this one dries out at low water, uncovering the meandering series of stepping stones making it possible to cross to the

eastern shore. Here reminders of the trading vessels that once provided a vital means of survival to fishermen and tradesmen lie, their ribs protruding through the muddy shore. Their ghostly skeletons etched along the coastline with echoes of their lives around them, where the voices of the seamen whisper to the sound of the surf.

South Hook

Further east from Sandy Haven is the site of the former Esso refinery which has now become the location of a Liquid Natural Gas facility. South Hook LNG chose the port as one of the deepest natural harbours in Europe and is one of the major providers of gas energy for the whole of the UK. At South Hook Point there is a former Victorian fort which was utilised by Esso when its refinery was in operation. This building was not the first fortification at the point however, as there is also evidence of an Iron Age earthwork promontory fort. It is staggering to consider that this site of such high technology has been involved in so many significant steps in the history of our island, where once foot soldiers stood guard over the Waterway now great ships land their precious cargoes.

Stack Fort and the Forts of the Haven

Stack Fort was one the range of further defensive improvements to the Haven following the 1858 "Report to Parliament on the Sea Defences of Milford Haven and Pembroke Dock."

Henry Temple, 3rd Viscount Palmerston, was responsible for this initiative. He advocated comprehensive fortifications systems at Portsmouth, Portland, Plymouth, Chatham and Milford Haven in view of any threat of invasion from the new Emperor, Napoleon III. Other forts were added at this time at Hubberston and Popton Point with between them a floating battery. By 1867 this created two lines of defence behind West Blockhouse, Dale and Thorn Island. Chapel Bay Fort built in 1899 rendered all others obsolete.

Stack Fort

Thorn Island

Angle

Esso refinery at South Hook in 1960.

At the village of Angle it became a tradition for the fishermen to paint their cottages various colourful hues. In addition to white, could be seen orange, blue and morning-glory, a colour named after the flower and prepared by mixing soot and pigs blood with limewash. The origin of this colourful display dates back to the late 19th Century when Colonel Mirehouse returned from the Boer War in South Africa. The Mirehouse family own the Angle Estate and had houses built and renovated in the traditional African style of the colonists. Flat roofs, castellations and rendered facades have given the village its unique appearance. Earlier inhabitants, the Anglo-Normans, built the Church of St Mary's here in the 13th Century with the red roof tiles as an addition, baked at the West Angle brickworks.

Reconstruction of the South Hook Terminal, 2007.

Angle Bay

Angle Churchyard

Among the graves at Angle Churchyard lie many British sailors, airmen, gunners, several Canadian airmen, one Polish airman and a Japanese sailor. This sailor was a crew member of the Hirano Maru, a Japanese merchant ship torpedoed off the Pembrokeshire coast in October 1918 by a German submarine UB91. For many years anonymous donations were sent annually to the Vicar of Angle with requests for flowers to be laid on the sailor's grave. A reminder of the love and grief expressed by an unnamed family member or loved one, who never saw the final resting place of this unfortunate sailor.

West Angle Bay

One stormy night in 1808 the HMS Leda strove desperately for shelter in Milford Haven, on board was Petty Officer Rixon, he was a local man who knew the area well, and as he realised that the ship was closing in on a dangerous reef he called frantically to the Captain to turn the ship around, but his pleas fell on deaf ears as the ship ran aground. Later timber was salvaged from hull, although guns and stores had all been lost. These timbers however were used to build a new Naval ship, the HMS Surprise.

Point House

Point House overlooking East Angle Bay dates from the 16th Century and local legends tell of a fire which burned continuously within the fireplace of the building for over two hundred years, the woody smells

The Point House, Angle

filling the interior of the building with warmth and comfort. At one time the landlord was a Customs Officer and he frequently housed John Callice, a notorious pirate who had an unusual intelligence on the expected arrival of certain ships. Callice then set out with his crew and plundered ships and cargo, the illicit gains were not only shared with the landlord of Point House but also with the Earl of Pembroke. Residing in Pembroke Castle, the Earl's rank was useful as insurance, he ensured that these lawbreakers were not apprehended or hindered in their dreadful, though lucrative business.★

Thorn Island

Sunset over Milford Haven

The Lifeboat

Even before the Lifeboat Station had been established, Silver Medals had been awarded to local men for the rescues of two brigantines and a schooner. In 1868 the RNLI had its first boathouse and a wooden slipway built on the eastern end of Angle Point, it was strengthened in 1888. In the late 1920s a new boathouse was constructed with a roller slipway, situated on the northern side of Angle Point. The lifeboat was hauled up the slipway bow first, and then manoeuvred on a turntable so it could be backed into the boathouse, ready for the next launch.

This was superceded by the present house and slipway in 1992, over 320 lives have been saved since 1868.

A Precious Cargo

The full-rigged ship Loch Shiel was outward bound from Glasgow, heading for Australia in January 1895. The ship encountered a ferocious gale, her Master decided to seek shelter in Milford Haven, under storm sails she made the harbour

Milford Haven in the 19th Century

entrance but in the hideous visibility in the heavy squalls of rain, the ship was turned too soon. Only a hundred yards or so and she would have missed Thorn Island and safely entered the estuary, the Angle lifeboat was launched and an heroic rescue ensued. The crew had managed to reach the island via the ship's bowsprit and all were saved, the Lifeboat crew were awarded commendations for their bravery. Walking out to see the wreck in the morning the villagers found much of the cargo scattered along the waters edge, not only general cargo but also desirable crates of whisky. The men of the village "liberated" all the whisky they could find for "safe keeping". When the Police and Customs Officers cordoned off the beach for the prevention of illicit salvage of the cargo other strategies were employed by the wily Angle men. Returning from walks along the beach empty-handed they had hidden caches of treasure in caves or holes in the cliffs. One father invented a new game for his little girl, she was able to walk past the policemen with a bottle fetched from this store neatly hidden in her bloomers under her long skirt, and the nice policemen smiled at her as she walked happily past. It appears that not much work was done by Angle men in the pursuing days, apart from sheer drunkenness several men died of alcoholic poisoning. There was a similar sad result near Milford when a case was discovered by two men, one staggered home after some sampling, the other was found two days later in a hedge having drunk himself to death. A father and son when attempting to tow a keg home from the wreck were both drowned when the boat capsized. Over many years well-hidden bottles would come to light during repairs to Angle cottages, and in the 1980s divers explored the wreck site retrieved yet another bottle, complete with contents.★

Thorn Island

Recently the buildings on Thorn Island were utilised as a hotel where earlier a hundred or so troops were stationed at this Victorian battery with nine guns positioned to defend the Haven.

The wreck of the Dakotian is marked by a buoy off Thorn Island, this liner was carrying general cargo including bicycles and Christmas puddings; intending to leave port on 21st November 1940 the ship was already underway when advised not to sail as the enemy was close by. On dropping anchor she was blown up by a magnetic mine, and sank in minutes.★

Milford Haven

The town of Milford Haven lies to the east of Gelliswick Bay on a headland overlooking the Waterway. The Frenchman, Jean Barrallier, from Toulon appointed as Inspector General of Naval Construction also concentrated his attention on planning out the town in a symmetrical grid iron pattern. There was no large supply of oak in the county so Milford may have seemed an unlikely choice for building ships.

The former Neyland to Pembroke Dock car ferry, Lady Margaret.

Naval Yard

Ship building skills fit for the Navy were available at Milford Haven, evident in a number of vessels produced in local yards including, in 1759, the first frigate Milford (28 guns). Charles Greville, nephew of Sir William Hamilton and manager of his estate, wished to build a new town called Milford Haven. To this end he encouraged the Royal Navy to build ships "in a yard here" and the Navy agreed with building commencing in 1800. Timing was apt as every ship was required during the war with France. Innovation also played a part, with the desire to take a fresh approach to shipbuilding.

Milford Dock fish market.

The Royal Navy had committed to Milford and seven warships followed. HMS Nautilus was built in 1804 and the following year had the task of conveying the news of Trafalgar and the death of Nelson into Lisbon. Another Milford (74 guns) was commissioned in 1809. Four years later the Navy's shipbuilding contract was transferred from the small yard at Milford to the Royal Dockyard, established at Paterchurch.★

The Great Eastern

Whaling

As well as establishing a shipbuilding industry for the town, another ambition was to set up a whaling centre from which spermaceti oil could be distributed to London for fuelling oil lamps. As gas lamps superceded those of oil, this trade rapidly declined.

The Great Eastern

When Brunel's Great Eastern berthed at Milford Haven his 690ft ship dwarfed buildings and cottages along the foreshore. Built by Messrs J. Scott Russell & Co of Milwall, the hull was laid down in May 1854 and launched on the last day of January 1858. Brunel was famously depicted by Howlett in a photograph taken in front of the huge launching chains. It would not be until 1899 that the Great Eastern was surpassed in length by the 750ft RMS Oceanic, and even later in tonnage, by RMS Celtic in 1901. Another Brunel ship, the Great Western, also appeared in the port. Size comparison can be made with another contemporary ship which survives today, Great Britain. Restored in Britain where she was built to Brunel's designs, her hull, not including the bowsprit is 322ft.

Disaster struck on the Great Eastern's first passage when off Hastings an explosion damaged the ship, and the No 1 funnel. Brunel's health was failing, and this news may have been a severe blow as he died some days afterwards on 15th September. Therefore he never heard of the success of his double hull construction a few years later when on her sixth voyage the Great Eastern hit an uncharted pinnacle rock off the New York coast. The damage included a massive hole torn in the outer hull, 83ft long and 9ft wide. Brunel's design saved the day, enabling the ship to reach New York.

After an earlier voyage from New York, departing on 17 August 1860 and sailing via Halifax, the Great Eastern arrived at Milford Haven on 29 August 1860.

An accident happened that winter when the ship was lying at Neyland having been on the grid for repairs to the propeller shaft. With the work complete and the ship ready for sea, she cast off her moorings, however a small sightseeing boat came too close and was caught up in the whirling propeller, the passengers screaming in fear as their boat was ripped apart, the great ship's engines were stopped sadly too late for two of the passengers that were sucked under beneath the waves. The tide caught the bow of the ship, swinging the Great Eastern in its current across the river towards the naval dockyard at Pembroke Dock. The Royal Naval frigate HMS Blenheim its paint gleaming, lying proudly at its mooring was sadly in the way and the Great Eastern crashed into it breaking spars and moorings to the consternation of the watching Admiralty.

After a voyage across the Atlantic and the ship was refitted as a troopship, crossing to Canada, from 1865 – 74 she became a cable-laying ship, firstly operating across the Atlantic to Newfoundland and later in the Indian ocean. In total thousands of miles of cable were laid from her decks before she was laid up at Milford Haven for twelve years becoming a part of the seascape.

HMS Andromeda, built at Pembroke Dock in 1897, 11,000 tons, became a training ship and renamed HMS Impregnable 1919, and HMS Defiance, 1931; scrapped 1956.

The Fishing Industry

Milford became the centre for the Welsh offshore fishing industry. Throughout the first half of the 20th Century it grew into the United Kingdom's fourth ranking fishing port with prime catches of hake, skate and conger. During this period an average of a hundred trawlers were operating on seven-to-fourteen day voyages. Such were the catches, that Milford residents boasted that each weekday was a pay-day, as the fishermen were noted for spending their hard earned income. Crew members received bonuses on top of their wages, a percentage of the net value of the trawler's catch. The amount varying according to their position in the crew. Even through the years of the Great Depression of the 1920s and 30s Milford sustained

FISH BOX FACTORY AT MILFORD DOCKS. (MILFORD HAVEN TIMBER AND BOX COMPANY.)

The Fish Market at Milford Docks

its busy and bustling quayside atmosphere. The peak year for the catch being 1946 when 60,000 tons of fish was landed. Sadly for the local population this prosperity was soon to end, already in the 1950s the decline was underway and by 1991 the old fish market was demolished. Currently a very small number of locally based vessels and a handful of other trawlers, principally from Belgium, manage to survive.

The Vikings

There is a hamlet near Dale called Hasguard Cross, a name it is believed that is derived from "Asgard", which was the home of the gods in Norse mythology. Islands and villages in Pembrokeshire have other

Norse names including Skomer, Skokholm, Ramsey, Solva and Freystrop (formerly Freyasdorp). Around the year 877 the chieftain Hubba and his Vikings, overwintered at Mid Fjord Havn. In local accounts the number of these ships varies from 23 to 200. However many, there are Viking roots in "Milford's Haven" and in Hubberston named after Hubba. A recent analysis made of descendents of Pembrokeshire families showed, through blood tests, convincing links to southern Scandinavia.

Stuns'ls set in the Indian ocean

Sea Stallion

The Icelandic Sagas also refer to Wales and raiding Vikings, these raids continued from 850 to 1100. Some settled peaceably as described in a translation of the "Burnt Njal", Kadi Solmundsson and Njal's sons "fared south to Wales and tarried there". Some raids were violent with Narberth being burnt in 998, and St David's attacked in 999 when Bishop Morgeneu was slain. On the last recorded raid in 1091 the Bishop Abraham, who was revered a Saint, lost his life. A large farm, established to the south of Pembroke became a settlement called Gander's Nest (in Norse gandir refers to a monster). Later this settlement was absorbed by a group of Normans led by Arnulf de Montgomery.

THE UPPER HAVEN

THE UPPER HAVEN

Pembroke

Pembroke's treasures include bronze age remains found at Monkton Bridge which are preserved in the collection at the National Museum of Wales. The sensitively restored Monkton Old Hall, which dates from the 15th Century and is privately owned, was originally the residence of the Prior. Arnulf de Montgomery, created Earl of Pembroke by King William II established the castle and the medieval Priory Church. Blessed with exceptional acoustics Monkton Priory has become a popular venue for concerts and recordings.

The striking features of the Chevron Refinery contrasts directly with the rolling Pembrokeshire countryside and its typical Haven scenery of sloping banks, bracken and blackthorn with old red sandstone soil adding to its distinctive colour.

Aerial shot of Pembroke

Pembroke Castle

Soon after the Battle of Hastings in 1066 the victorious Norman invaders advanced towards Wales building castles at Chepstow and later, Cardiff. Following this progression westwards as it was in 1093 that Arnulf de Montgomery started to build the first Pembroke Castle. Unlike the stone of Chepstow this castle started with a fairly basic structure of timber palisades, which still stood firm against Welsh counter attacks, successfully withstanding two sieges. It's strategic importance growing as Pembroke became the base for the Normans' campaigns in Ireland.

William Marshall, an advisor to King John concerning the Magna Carta, became Regent to the infant king, Henry III. He continued building the castle at Pembroke with the Great Tower and sections of the Inner Ward with further construction occurring between 1234 and 1241 by his third son Gilbert.

Later on the castle became the property of William de Valence who was a half-brother of Henry III and married Joan, granddaughter of William Marshall. His family retained ownership for 70 years extending the walls and towers around the outer ward. They also paid attention to the town's defences providing walls and three main gateways.

Henry Tewdwr & The Tudor Dynasty

Years later the Castle came into possession of a newly created Earl, who made it more home fortification. Finer details were added including an oriel window. This new owner was Henry VI's half-brother, Jasper Tewdwr, Earl of Pembroke whose 15 year-old sister-in-law, Margaret, was sent to the castle for her safety during the Wars of the Roses. It was here she gave birth to a son, Henry Tewdwr, in 1457. None other than the founder of the Tudor dynasty who was forced into exile in Brittany during the Wars of the Roses.

Pembroke Castle

Returning with his uncle, Jasper, he landed with 2000 men at Mill Bay in 1485 and joined by other followers, marched with the flag of Cadwallader's red dragon alongside the flag of St George. Richard III was defeated at Bosworth Field with Henry crowned Henry VII, King of England and Wales. He never returned to Pembroke where he had grown up, or even to Wales, but nevertheless the links were not lost and his son Henry's titles included Prince of Wales and Earl of Pembroke.

Destruction and Restoration

During the Civil War the Castle endured a seven-week siege by the Roundheads led by Cromwell who on its capitulation ordered its destruction. The siege of this otherwise impregnable castle was brought to an end only by the discovery, and the subsequent denial to the defenders, of its underground water supply. With the ruins neglected, ivy ran rampant over the walls until 1880 when a gentleman from Brecon, Mr J R Cobb, spent three years making a start to rescue what remained. Almost fifty years later work began again led by General Sir Ivor Phillips of Cosheston Hall who added it to his property portfolio in 1928. This intensive project has been satisfactorily completed with the result that most of the towers and walls are returned to what they were like in the Middle Ages and it is maintained today by a trust.

Pembroke Dock Gun Tower

Crow Pool

The Waterway from Milford Haven to Cleddau Bridge is largely industrialised on both sides. Pennar Mouth, a gap in the ridge that divides Pembroke from the main estuary, leads to Crow Pool which lies within the Gut. Now running due east, the river lies behind the ridge with gently sloping farmland to the south contrasting with the modern housing development on the steep north shore. Although the river is nearly half a mile wide at high tide only a narrow channel flows through the mud along the northern shore at low water.

Crow Pool

From Jacob's Pill to Japan

The private yard at Jacob's Pill won an impressive order from the Imperial Japanese Navy in 1874. A 2200 ton corvette was laid down in September 1875 and was launched as the Hiei in June 1877. This ship, named after Mount Hiei outside Kyoto and commissioned in the next year, arrived in Japan with a British crew in May 1888. Later she would undertake a number of extended training cruises to India and further west to the Mediterranean, before taking part in the First Sino-Japanese War, when she received some damage at the battle of Yalu River in 1894 and finally was broken up in 1911. Lt. Hechahiro Togo her first commanding officer sent a gingko tree to Pembroke Dock as a token of his appreciation for kindness during his stay while supervising the ships construction, now over a hundred years old, the tree is still surviving. Lieutenant Togo, later Admiral, became supreme commander of the fleet which defeated the Chinese in 1894 and the Russians in 1905.

This same small yard which built Hiei won the order to build HMS Acorn, launched in June 1884, and also construct the dock gates for Milford Dock. Completed in 1887 these gates lasted for one hundred and three years, only being replaced in 1990.★

While ship building has long ceased, Mitec, part of Pembrokeshire College keeps boat building and marine engineering skills alive through accredited training courses and maintenance and restoration work on traditional vessels is carried out by West Wales Maritime Heritage Society in its workshop.

Hazelbeach

As early as 1594 records show that Haselbytch, as it was then known was regarded as a "good riding for ships and a good anchor hold…" Situated on the north shore of the Haven the village of Hazelbeach opens up after passing Wear Point. During the 17th 18th and 19th centuries the beach near Wear Point was a source of constant activity with smaller cargo ships transferring coal, grain, culm and limestone to horses and carts for local delivery. There is an impressive stone quay remaining from these earlier times maintained by the Hazelbeach Boat Club as their boatyard. It is believed that a pier extended into the waterway in former times, providing access at all states of the tide, but nowadays a pontoon jetty allows small vessels to come alongside for several hours either side of high water.

Neyland Railway Terminus

In 2006 Neyland celebrated the bicentenary of the birth of Isambard Kingdom Brunel with few in Wales claiming so close a relationship with this great engineer. Brunel chose Neyland as the destination of the railway route from Haverfordwest to the Waterway and an Act of Parliament cemented his plan. Passed in 1852 this Act changed the destiny of the 250 inhabitants of Neyland and for those days this was a dramatic event for a quiet village. Brunel is recorded as trialling the route in a light train with fellow engineers in January 1856 before the line was opened three months later. From that date sprang a constant flow of inward migration creating businesses, shops, accommodation, inns and chapels, along with other signs of progress. Brunel returned a number of times and played a significant role promoting trade in the area. The Spring of 1857 saw further activity and excitement when a pontoon to his design was launched at Neyland. Its huge dimensions allowed easier boarding and loading for passengers and livestock, for the next fifty years Neyland was a hub for communications, with the ferry linking Wales with Waterford and Cork, but this service ended when the cross channel ferry transferred to Fishguard in 1906.

I. K Brunel - statue at Neyland

RAF Pembroke Dock

Pembroke Dock and the Royal Navy

The settlement at Paterchurch grew substantially from 1814 when the Admiralty established its ship yard. Originally to be called Melville Town it turned out otherwise as consignments of goods delivered to the dockyard were marked "For Pembroke Dock" which by common usage became adopted for the whole town. The first two ships constructed were the frigates Ariadne and Valorous, launched on the same day in 1816. HMS Erebus was completed in 1826, having both sails and steam power. Under the command of Sir John Franklin their names would become synonymous with the difficulties and tragedies of the search for the North West Passage.

Notable ships built at the Royal Dockyard include Tartarus in 1834, the yard's first steam warship, and HMS Gorgon of 1837 which was the Royal Navy's first really successful steam warship.

HMS Conflict of 1846 was their first propeller-driven warship while HMS Lion, launched in 1847 was at that time the largest ship in the Royal Navy. The first rate, HMS Howe, with 110 guns was the largest and the last three-decker ever built, one of 250 ships built at Pembroke Dock HMS Howe was launched in 1860.

By the 1860s the yard was in danger of becoming obsolete following the development of the iron-clad warships, however, skilled craftsmen at the yard were conversant in working with iron, and so workers from other dockyards came to Pembroke Dock to learn iron-working skills. Side by side with the ironclads there evolved the composite ship composed of wooden planking on iron frames. The yard was constantly adapting techniques for building with iron and steel used for the construction of gun-boats and other small craft. Among other vessels built at Pembroke were seven Royal Yachts, three bearing the name Victoria and Albert.★

In the past there were plenty of passengers for local ferries, with routes across this part of the Waterway including Pembroke Ferry/Burton, Burton/Neyland, and Bentlass near Hundleton to Ferry Road at Pembroke Dock. The latter was the scene of a tragedy in 1889 when one stormy morning a number of women returning with their purchases from the market at Pembroke Dock where tragically drowned when Bentlass ferry capsized. Their long heavy woollen skirts filled with water and dragged them under. The Neyland to Hobbs Point ferry prospered at the expense of the traditional Pembroke Ferry to Burton route.

Today's ferry, the Isle of Inishmore, seen from Angle

Sunderland Flying Boats

Four years after the Royal Dockyard had closed, the RAF arrived at Pembroke Dock with a unit of one officer with a handful of men. More followed and for almost three decades the waters of Milford Haven echoed to the sound of aero engines shattering the silence of the sheltered waters of the haven. The succession of flying-boats began with the Southampton twin-engined open cockpit biplanes. In the early days development was tentative and took place amidst the crippling unemployment of the early 30s but gradually the appearance of the former dockyard was changed when a suitable slipway was constructed together with two large hangars which are still prominent landmarks. The Southamptons were replaced in turn by Rangoons, Singapores, Stranraers and finally

Sunderlands and Catalinas. The sound of which became a familiar part of local life, with take offs and landings weaving a pattern on the air and on the water.

Known as PD, by its initials, Pembroke Dock became a favourite posting for the elite flying-boat personnel and with war clouds looming over Europe the base became vital to help guard the trade routes of the Western Approaches.

Pembroke Dock became the largest flying-boat station in the world and at a peak time in the mid-war years 99 flying-boats, mainly Sunderlands or Catalinas, were moored in or around the Haven. Accommodating so many was a challenge.

Sunderland Flying-Boat

There are a few local reminders of this rare chapter of flying history in Pembrokeshire. A memorial plaque unveiled at St. John's Church by the distinguished flying-boat pilot, Air Vice-Marshall Donald Bennet in 1985, commemorated the town's flying-boat links. This occurred during the first flying-boat reunion, which have been followed by the other reunions ensuring memories of the endeavours of those who flew and serviced the squadron lives on.

Of all the 749 military Sunderland flying-boats built only three survive, exhibited in museums in New Zealand and the UK. These are Mark V versions, dating from the end of World War II. However one of the Mark I remains extant in 2008 hidden from view, on the seabed between Pembroke Dock and Neyland. Identified as serial number T9044 of 210 Squadron which sank in a gale at her mooring in November 1940 without loss of life. It was many years before the plane was located by divers and subsequently a recovery programme adopted. At that time one of its Pegasus radial engines, having been raised from the wreck, was

RAF Pembroke Dock, with Sunderlands on the ground.

A Sunderland airborne.

being restored ashore with plans advancing rapidly to recover this unique wartime survivor and to conserve and display it as the initial centrepiece of an exhibition centre in Pembroke Dock. Thus telling the remarkable story of flying-boats and their key hole in the long running Battle of the Atlantic – one of the major campaigns of World War II.

The Pegasus engine already recovered is in the ownership of the Pembroke Dock Sunderland Trust, whose dedicated volunteers worked long hours on its conservation while other examples of their workmanship are on display at the Gun Tower Museum in Front Street, Pembroke Dock. Pembroke Dock Sunderland Trust acknowledges the great support received from Milford Haven Port Authority including the protection of the wreck site by a 100 metre exclusion zone.

END OF PART ONE

PART TWO

THE DAUGLEDDAU

THE DAUGLEDDAU

The confluence of the Eastern and Western Cleddau rivers is known as Daugleddau.
This is the area of water from the Cleddau Bridge to Picton Point.

Burton

Immediately above Cleddau Bridge is the village of Burton which was the location of several small shipyards during the 18th and 19th centuries, including Dean's Shipyard next to the Jolly Sailor. Amongst a dozen ships built here was the two masted schooner, Fanny Ann, built in 1858 and 63ft long. Trading to Liverpool and Ireland, on one trip one of her masts was carried away and a new one fitted on Kilrush. Sailing the Galway coast in 1863, she was wrecked on the island of Aran but all the crew were saved.★

Billy Darkie's Ferry

The ferry from Neyland Steps to Barnstable was operated from 1908-1938 by William Griffiths who was known as Billy Darkie. This was a popular route, linking the railway at Neyland with the village of Burton. Contracts held with the Post Office and Trinity House ensured steady traffic and a regular income while school children had a special weekly rate. On duty from early morning until ten at night, Billy always rowed standing up, facing the direction in which he was heading. Anyone trying to break into Billy's monopoly felt the wrath of this normally quiet man. His method of stopping the competition involved opening seacocks in the moored boats of the would-be rival ferrymen during the night.★★

Trinity House Jetty

A large timber jetty was built by Trinity House to enable service vessels to berth at this depot for materials, replenishment and rest when taking care of the buoys, lighthouses and light vessels in this coastal district. Originally known as Trinity Yachts, tenders operated from Burton during the first part of the 20th Century. Until the closure of the depot in 1926 when the operation was transferred to Swansea.

HMS Warrior

For many years, opposite Burton lay the Royal Navy's first iron warship, HMS Warrior. What was a vessel of advanced design for the period with massive cannon range, and more than a match for the French La Gloire. In latter years her proud past was forgotten when she served as a humble jetty for the Ministry of

The Warrior - refurbished and currently at Portsmouth

Defence oil storage depot, a deployment which prevented an early voyage to the shipbreaker. Thus this treasure of the past was rescued, and after undergoing major restoration, was given a prominent berth near the HMS Victory at Portsmouth.

Cosheston

A network of ferries criss-crossed the Haven to provide a daily service while saving many miles of uncomfortable road travel. One such ferry-boat operated from Cosheston across the Cresswell River to Lawrenny, and then over the Daugleddau River to Rhoose near Benton Castle. This appears to have been government-owned as soldiers, policemen and postmen travelled free of charge while other passengers paid two old pence for Lawrenny to Cosheston trip with thrupence for the Lawrenny to Rhoose ferry ride crossing the main Daugleddau river, this being the only income for the ferrymen.*

Canton's shipyard, shown on the Admiralty chart of 1845, was on the southern shore of the Cresswell River, the slipway it once used can still be seen from the quay at Lawrenny. Ships were also built on the

Cosheston Pill

Rhoose, near Benton, from Cosheston [landing place for ferry] from Lawrenny and Cosheston

shore west of Canton's Yard by Thomas Howell, a Neyland shipwright who married Mary Howell, the daughter of a Pembroke Dock builder. From before the 1860s the couple as Morgan and Howells went on to run a chemical works producing naptha and other chemicals for explosives, which mainly were sold to a company in Neath. Their house and the building used for the chemical works can best be seen from the river.★

Beach close to site of Canton's Shipyard, Cosheston

Whalecombe, formerly Morgan and Howell's Chemical Works, Cosheston.

Williamston Pill

The area around Williamstone Pill was once an extensive limestone quarry, begun in the 16th Century and later supplying stone to the Haven fortifications. The limestone was cut and loaded directly into lighters for shipping downstream to the forts along the Haven. Limestone was also burnt for agricultural and structural purposes in hundreds of kilns up and down the whole Waterway system, and around the coasts of West Wales. It is difficult to visualise today the noise and bustle which must have occurred in its heyday but this network is now deserted with only the remains of old vessels to remind one of the past. One of the vessels used in coastal trading, the ketch Boy Harry, lies abandoned in the mud, remnants of her timbers being exposed at low water, her ancient oil engine a rusting heap of iron are all that remains to this, a carvel built vessel of only 20 tons which had

Quarry at West Williamston, with wreck (thought to be "Boy Harry").

a transom stern. Barnacled remains of other sailing vessels abandoned years ago lie in a nearby basin among which is the Alice and Charles Pierce.

Wreck of 'Morning Glory' a former trawler at Lawrenny

Benton Castle

Benton Castle

Lawrenny

The Carew and Creswell Rivers meet at Lawrenny, this once busy port was crucial to the lime trade where ferries bustled back and forth to Cosheston and Rhoose Ferry across the main Cleddau waterway. A slipway built in the Second World War was used also by Walrus flyingboats, and stories are told of local children that were given joy rides up and down the river in them. Even today that same slipway is the centre of boating activity, busy with dinghies setting forth for family fishing outings and children splashing in and out of the river along the pebbled shoreline.

Three Walrus of 764 Squadron Fleet Air Arm

Up river from Lawrenny, on the eastern bank of the Cleddau River are the Hanging Woods, a National Trust property through which a footpath winds clinging to the bank, to the next inlet of Garron Pill. On the northern shore of this quiet shady creek a number of channels can be found disappearing into hidden flooded quarries, where birds flit and swoop overhead, wildlife abounding, watching you from above.

Lawrenny

Cresswell River

At the confluence of the Cresswell and Carew rivers, clearly visible as the tide goes out, lies the Black Mixen (or Misken, for local derivations of midden). This mound was created by ballast discharged from ships prior to loading stone or coal at Cresswell Quay. The coal mined in the Pembrokeshire Coalfield, was brought down in barges and stored in a pound that can still be seen today opposite the Cresselly Arms Public House and at Bevan's Yard was situated on the north shore of the Cresswell River at Lawrenny, where it was transferred into larger sea going vessels. Coal mined locally at Jeffreston and Cresselly was mainly delivered to ports along the Bristol Channel, a busy trade in the mid 18th Century.

River barges capable of carrying about 30 tons of coal, with a single mast and a big square sail known as Willy Boys were crewed by one man and a boy. Their skill enabled them to use the fierce tides to advantage, using large sweeps or oars to regulate the manoeuvres. Interestingly, instead of using the terms "port" and "starboard" their local terminology was "bucket" and "broom" determined from the side of the ship these were stowed.

Quarries and Limestone

Arthur Clague, who died in 1987, left a great legacy for future generations through his memories of trade and trading vessels.

"I remember Fred John of Cresswell Quay and myself, taking a cargo of limestone from the quarries opposite Llangwm, to Robert Warlow's kilns at Haverfordwest. We were in the William & Emma which was a ketch rigged with a single cylinder Brit auxiliary engine.

We loaded thirty five tons of stone, and after checking that it was properly trimmed, we started the engine and motored out of the quarry into the main channel, when the water gasket burst and stopped the engine.

Cresswell Quay, painted by Lady Catherine Allen (courtesy Mr. Tom Lloyd)

Fred got the anchor down and I set about repairing the leak by cutting a new gasket, and sealing the joint with soapy string.

The Brit had a huge flywheel which I started to swing to re-start it, but it kicked back and knocked me across the deck and up against the bulkhead. As I was the engineer on board, and in no condition to repeat the exercise, we decided to hoist the sails, and I got up the foresails, main and mizzen, and sailed her up passed Landshipping Quay, but got stuck on a sandbank opposite Millin Pill.

The tide was now ebbing, so we put the anchor in the punt and dropped it out in the channel, and settled down for the night, waiting for the morning tide. At sunrise we winched her out into the channel and as the river above Hook is too narrow to sail a vessel of that size, we lashed the helm, and took to the punt, with both Fred and I rowing. However, the flood tide took charge, and the William & Emma passed us by, fouling the moorings of several compass net boats at Little Milford before going aground below Crane's wood.

We spent a second night aboard, and with the aid of the winch and two fourteen foot poles which we kept on board, we got her going again the following morning. Approaching the narrows, the Mary Jane Lewis came up behind us and offered us a tow which we were pleased to accept; casting us off at the Gas Quay where we were due to discharge."

An interview by Barrie Burgess, local historian from 'The Secret Waterway' (WWMHS)
N.B. Barrie Burgess records the total distance travelled in three days was less than ten miles.

Carew

The Carew river is fairly wide and shallow, similar to that of Cresswell, from where trade is recorded with Newfoundland in as early as 1566 with the barque Perrot, named after and owned by Sir John Perrot of Carew. This trade route, also including France, continued during 1600-1603 aboard the 100 ton Lion of Milford.

Carew Castle

At the end of the 11th century an Anglo-Norman baron, Gerald de Windsor, was warden of Pembroke Castle on behalf of Henry I when he decided to build his own fortification on the Carew River. Much of what remains today was the work of Sir Nicholas Carew who died in 1311. Finally Sir John Perrot (1530-1592) was responsible for an extensive addition to the medieval castle which included the section with the large windows overlooking the mill pond.

Carew Castle and French Tidal Mill

French Tidal Mill

The French tidal mill and the castle which are maintained under the stewardship of Pembrokeshire Coast National Park Authority was constructed by French prisoners captured during the Napoleonic wars who were held at Pembroke in the Golden Prison, from where they were marched to Carew. A dam constructed across the creek allowed the tide to flow in until high water, with the outgoing tide controlled by sluices to turn the wheel which provided power to the mill. This dam, and another at Pembroke, have sufficient width to be useful as bridges for access while cargo vessels had water enough to reach the mills at high water. This enabled the constant cycle of delivering corn and loading flour for delivery or sale although the ships had to dry out on the mud and await the next tides.

Longer vessels at Pembroke could not berth directly beside the mill utilising the North Quay in its stead. David James recounts how a relative, who was about five foot tall and known as Annie of the Mill, helped to unload the cargoes. Managing with ease she carried two-hundred weight sacks up the steep narrow gangplanks to the shore.★

Carew Castle and French Tidal Mill

Llangwm

Llangwm, with a long seafaring tradition whose inhabitants has roots in mixed Viking and Flemish ancestry, is the only sizeable village on the upper reaches of the Waterway, where it is situated at the head of a short pill here which subdivides into two shallower inlets. Traditionally the fishermen caught bass, herring, mullet, salmon and sewin, from small tarred boats, and also harvested oysters and cockles. Their catches were sold by the womenfolk, travelling as far as Haverfordwest and Tenby, using donkeys and carts to carry the fare, but went on foot to the local markets.

Black Tar, Llangwm

LLANGWM FISHWOMAN.

Llangwm Women

Observers noted in the nineteenth Century that the women of Llangwm showed remarkable individualism, unique to the area. Beyond their industrious nature they held a sense of aloofness from other of the local communities, maintaining a reserve hard to penetrate. Until the end of the 19th Century they had a particular style of dress, wearing relatively short petticoats and jackets. These were often pea-jackets, or "my man's jacket", as they would say. This more practical clothing meant they were freer and less encumbered, for the hard rigours of their daily work for which the conventional styles were not so obliging.

Said to be hardy and industrious with a fair and bright appearance they were also noted as being, not infrequently, decidedly attractive. Being neither shy, nor immodest, they communicated easily, relating to all classes of society with an appealing frankness. AS young girls they would never be allowed to go into service and as for marriage only men from the village were eligible. Some have recorded that it was the custom for a man to take his wife's surname, henceforward being known by both his wife's and his own name. This did not work in reverse as it was uncommon for the wife to take her husband's.

Black Tar

In the Victorian era Black Tar was the focal point of Waterway activity on this section of the river, and so it remains today. Many fishing boats operated from its shore, and records exist of a number of kelpers' kilns. It is also thought to have been the place of embarkation for reinforcements and supplies to the Roundheads during their unsuccessful siege of Picton Castle.

Culm

A small open-cast mine was situated in Knap Wood near to Black Tar, villagers would work in this compound for its culm. Mixed with clay and water, anthracite dust was formed into small balls the size of a goose egg. Families were known to work together, wearing clogs for treading the mix, after which they hand crafted it into balls. This fuelled domestic fires and lime kilns with an intense slow burning heat.

Hideaways

Nowadays people discover hidden places for a relaxed and sometimes romantic pastime. In earlier days there was more anxiety when young men of the village sought the seclusion of Knap Wood mine. On such occasions the tension must have been tremendous as they sought to elude the might of naval press gangs with hiding away in the further reaches of the creeks of the Upper Haven was another option. But how to know when the coast was clear again was another matter. In this landscape far away from the sandy beaches, cliff-tops and vast expanses of deep water at the entrance and Lower Haven, are steep wooded banks, low meadows and sheltered pills overhung by trees, filled with undergrowth, a haven for wildlife. But those avoiding the Press Gangs, whose capture meant sailing the high seas often never to return, here was an ideal hiding place.

Limekiln at Cosheston Ferry; lime, burnt with culm as fuel, was used to fertilise agricultural land

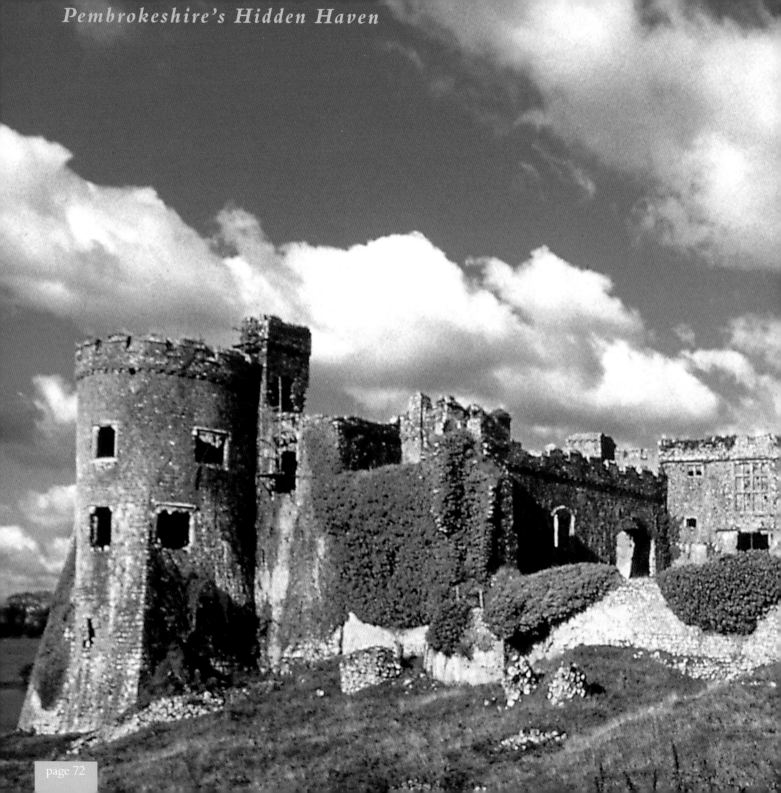

Carew Castle

THE RIVERS

THE RIVERS

The Eastern Cleddau

From the late medieval period through to the early 20th Century the Eastern Cleddau was alive with shipping, it was the most practical way to move around. Small craft criss-crossed from shore to shore, many families having their own boats while also using the ferry routes. These ferries were powered by oars until small motors became affordable. All the way down the Cleddau ferries carried different types of cargo, an essential link to the rest of Pembrokeshire. It was a small part of such a busy waterway where so much life evolved around it.

Looking up-river with Pembroke Dock in the foreground.

Landshipping

A gentle breeze skated down the Cleddau where a large ketch drifted down the river, the sails flapped loudly as the winds dropped and lifted again. A cargo ship carrying essential trade to Haverfordwest, taking a long patient journey along the river. Where Captains and crew watched carefully before them at the dangers that lurked beneath the water, where jagged rocky points threatened the completion of such a long journey and the tidal currents deciding on the eventual fate of each ship. It was a time when trade depended entirely upon the deadly will of the river.

At this point the Cleddau split into two, one direction to Canaston and the other to the busy market town of Haverfordwest.

Coal Mining

Even in the depths of the coal mine in the early 19th Century in Landshipping the river could be heard above, the sound of the ships passing over them, an eerie prospect for many workers. Even underground the lives of men and boys were decided by the hands of the river, when Mother Nature once again showed how fragile the hold mankind had over the strength of her rivers. One fateful day 42 men never returned home after drowning deep in the mine shafts and the mine soon became abandoned in 1845. Today the mine has crumbled and only the ghosts of the tram lines remain and those forgotten souls who still haunt the shoreline in the mist.

Picton Castle

Picton Castle

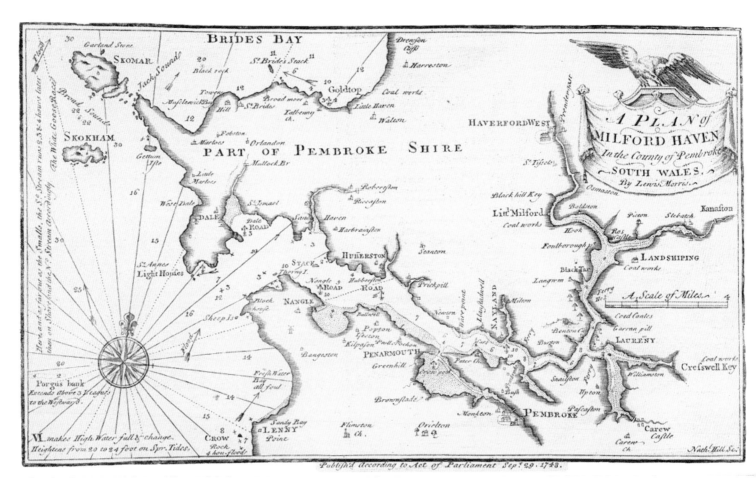

The Lewis Morris chart of Milford Haven, 1743

Straight from romantic novels stands Picton Castle, a proud addition to the vast plethora of castles within Pembrokeshire. However where other castles add only to the historical background of the county as a whole Picton Castle tells a tale of a strong family bond and its strength since 1420 to keep the castle within the name of the Philipps family.

During the Civil War the castle was taken siege by the Royalists, the Philipps family fought to defend their association with the Parliamentarians and their castle, losing it only momentarily to win it back with a clever tactic, proving their strength and passion to keep their beloved home. Today the Philipps family still keep residence in the castle and the building has doubled in size since its original construction. The gardens have been maintained to boast delightful displays of azaleas and rhododendrons.

Heronry

The woods in Picton provide a cooling retreat for those rambling along the rugged coastline, where the sound of lapping water brings you back to nature regardless of when in history you lived, the untouched beauties and secrets casting stories and whispers around you. Where only the wildfowl and wading birds are your companions and the legendary heron would sometimes grace you with his regal presence as if he himself should belong in the castle not far from his quiet retreat.

Wizo-the-Fleming

Early in the 12th Century Wizo-the-Fleming received land as a gift from King Henry I, at the end of the first Crusade in 1099 the Flemish foundation of the Hospital of St John of Jerusalem established a commandery (hospital) at Slebech. Wizo's Flemish followers, arriving after 1108, proved able with both the plough and sword. Settling over a wider area, Wizo and his men had the courage and skill necessary of the time in order to maintain control. This ability and character was given forthright praise by the most patriotic of Welshmen, Geraldus Cambrensis, who travelled widely at the end of the 12th Century.

Slebech Hall

As the river snakes its way towards Canaston you can glimpse remains of buildings, a reminder of the rich history that Pembrokeshire bestows and the trades that the county provided from the usage of the river. Ketches carrying grain once were carried up this twisting river past the grand buildings that once were Slebech Hall, now only foundations and rubble, onwards past the islands marking the final resting places of the Knights Templar, through the woods to their final destination Blackpool Mill, hidden in the depths of the trees around it. The Mill still stands, although no longer producing flour, like it once did in its hey day.

Western Cleddau

There is a thousand year history of trade on the Western Cleddau, around 900AD a small group of Vikings settled at the highest point navigable on the river.

The hall and towers at Slebech

Hook - Coal Mining

Anthracite was mined at Hook for centuries being most productive during the 19th Century, when Hook's Colliery provided a significant contribution of 29 percent of all the anthracite mined in Wales. Transportation was by barge or small coastal steamers until the railway linked Hook with Johnson. Above Fowborough Point there are remnants of at least two quays from those days of bustling coal-trade, although today they are barely used, one completely obliterated and the other grassed over and used mainly by local boatmen. A tree-covered cliff rises some 50m above the winding river at the foot of which are the remains of what was once a substantial jetty from where anthracite was shipped. Reaching the jetty involved the use of a Heath Robinson contraption, an inclined plane, which emptied the anthracite into the holds of lighters and coasters. Large vessels were unable to use these berths, so were anchored off Llangwm where the lighters could load them.

When the last pit closed in 1952 it was not the death knell of the village as it had been of so many other Welsh mining communities, here most of the miners frequently combined their pit work with time spent on smallholdings and fishing, thus aiding their survival when the coal was gone.

Blackpool Mill

Millin

A honey bee buzzes energetically on the bank of this little creek, sniffing at the flowers nestled on the banks around it. The rich sweet smell of the bluebells in early spring, is this where the precious taste of Pembrokeshire Honey comes from, bottled nectar of the sweet scent of spring, encapsulating the vista before it. Through the trees the river glistens in the sun millions of tiny crystals in the water glittering back at you through the glimpses between the trees. The near perfect reflection of the trees in the river cast back an alternate world within the depth of the river. Soon the moon will bathe the banks with a cooling crisp light, lighting up the creek for the nocturnal creatures of the night, even then the creek will refuse to sleep with the world around it.

Little Milford

Ballast from the colliers was perpetually being dumped at Little Milford and Hook, this created areas nowadays identified as grass-covered mounds near to the riverbank. The river follows a tortuous route from Hook, narrowing suddenly at Hook Bight, before swinging due north, this area of the river was the domain of the compass net fishermen.

Compass Netting

Suited to rivers where there are fast-flowing tidal currents, this method of fishing was introduced to the

Waterway over two hundred years ago by two Gloucestershire men, Ormond and Edwards. They had

come to Pembrokeshire to work in the Landshipping coalmine.

In this method of fishing the boat is held stationary in mid-stream by ropes rigged fore and aft, these are secured to stakes driven into the mud banks on the shoreline, placed at the narrowest points of the two rivers. Bag shaped nets are used to fish, these nets are called compass nets. With the boat moored, the nets are fastened to an A-shaped frame made of two

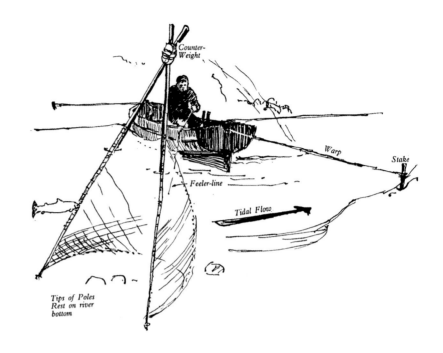

poles which are connected to a cross-piece resting on the river bed and leaning against the boat. The fisherman waits, still and patient, for the ripping tide to seep the fish into the net. Traditionally, the boat was a 14ft carvel rowing boat which had been tarred. Larch was usually used for the long poles that made up the frames, this timber had been buried for long periods in the shoreline mud to harden and prepare it for use.

Three hours after the beginning of the ebb was the crucial time, the only window when fishing was possible. During the 19th Century up to a hundred men from Hook and Llangwm were fishing commercially in this manner, although today this skill has virtually died out except for one or two men. One of the last compass fishing boats, K3, is preserved by the West Wales Maritime Heritage Society.

Black Hill Quay

Heading northwards from Hook lie the tree covered remains of Black Hill Quay with its limekiln, wildfowl are abundant with heron, greenshank, shelduck, curlew, little egret and flocks of Canada geese.

Following a sweeping left hand bend the river turns north-west at the White Rock, the boundary of the port of Haverfordwest which lies 28 miles from St Ann's Head.

Haroldston Hall

Approaching by sea the river winds by saltings, the sites of bygone quarries and old quays. In the valley of Merlin Brook stands the ruins of the Tudor mansion of Haroldston. During the 16th and 17th centuries this was the home of the Perrot family whose royal connection lay with Sir John Perrot, the bastard son of Henry VII. Renowned in the area as a great benefactor, the charity he bestowed on the town continues to this day.

The present Haroldston House was built in Georgian times and has Victorian additions, where a paper mill once stood now stands a mineral water factory. This spring water is sourced from Higgons Well and is piped under the river. Ancient Gothic stonework still covers the well which is fed by a copious spring which no doubt supplied water to the ships of times gone by. Bridges now thwart the entrance of vessels with high masts into Haverfordwest.

Haroldston Hall

Gas Works Quay, Haverfordwest

Once a hub of activity, large ships arrived with flour at the warehouses on the quay. Steamers, like the Ben Rein worked with a crew of only 3 on the tides to the Gasworks Quay unloading its cargo to supply the town.

Right up to the latter years of trading sail, topsail schooners could come alongside with a variety of cargoes and even cement was delivered from Milford to Skinners Wharf.

SS Gleniffer at Gas Quay, Haverfordwest. Capt. John George and Gwillym George.

Haverfordwest

The port of Haverfordwest lies at the heart of Pembrokeshire; this county town is rich with history from the castle ruins and mediaeval churches to ballustraded town-house terraces and Georgian architecture. Approaching by sea the river winds past saltings, the sites of bygone quarries and old quays.

Haverfordwest life, including trade by steam grew during the 14th and 15th centuries, thus it was in 1479 that Edward, Prince of Wales, under the direction of his father, King Edward VI, issued the town's charter. With this came the right to appoint a Mayor who also acted as the Admiral of the Port of Haverfordwest. This powerful man could: "Grant and make letter of safe conduct to all manner of foreign aliens under league, treaty, friendship or safe conduct of the King who should come with their merchandise into Milford."

Haverfordwest

Trade flourished during the next two centuries when the port handled a great variety of goods to and from various ports in Europe. Outgoing trade included wool, hides, friezes (rough woollen cloth), corn, coal, culm, different types of Welsh cloth and various fish. Among the incoming goods were textiles, leather, foodstuffs, hardware, wine, oil, flour, fruit and iron. As the merchants prospered the town flourished.

The changing economy

The decline in commerce began when the Civil Wars (1642-1648) and the Plague (1652) had grievous effects upon trade thus harming the economy of Haverfordwest, the next two centuries brought recovery, but later, with construction of larger ships in excess of 200 tons meant that ships could not navigate into the port. This, along with the lack of positive action by the port authorities, combined with the growth of

Gasometer collapse in Haverfordwest 1901.

technology promoted the decline. Already by 1830, maintenance of the river was so neglected that the accumulation of silt restricted access to vessels with a maximum draft of 10ft or up to 100 tons. Plans to improve the Western Cleddau were drawn up in 1843 but never implemented, and it became increasingly

uneconomic to maintain the harbour and its related port services.

In 1853, the railway reached the town producing an alternative means of transportation, additionally after the First World War, as roads improved, vehicles were used more and more. By the 1930s all trade to Haverfordwest by sea had ceased.

Pirates

In days gone by Ship Street was lined with fine stone warehouses, alive with commercial and maritime activity. Inns and lodging houses were frequented by sailors from many ships which through the centuries tied up alongside the quays.

All the profitable trade acted like a magnet and two notable pirates made their headquarters at Haverfordwest. Robert Hicks and John Callice frequented Ship Street (now known as Quay Street) where they sold their cargo, brought from their ships, to the townspeople and merchants. Laden with timber, rye

Pembrokeshire-born pirate, Barti Ddu.

and salt everything sold rapidly in the town, whilst the poorer people bought rye and the more prosperous, the wheat. Such was their stronghold over the street that townspeople were afraid to walk down Ship Street because of the ferocious nature of these pirates; it is believed that the street is still haunted by the ghosts of these men. Hicks and Callice were known to lodge with Richard Merchant, an innkeeper and merchant.

Another pirate who often sailed into the Haven was Herberd aboard the Elephant, whose cargoes included salt, wheat, rye, dried fish and wine from Gascony. The latter, being expensive, was bought by a select clientele while there was a ready market for most other commodities. Sir John Perrot was one of the leading citizens thought to have lent support to the pirates. Admiralty officials, customs officers as well as civic dignitaries such as the mayors of Haverfordwest, Pembroke and Tenby all had dealings with pirates.

Beating the Bounds

The mayors also held the office of Admiral of the Port, handed down through the centuries. Each summer the current mayor, in Admiral's role, officiates at the ancient ceremony of Beating the Bounds. Travelling by river launch he is escorted by members of the town council followed by numerous citizens and visitors.

The route to the White Rock and back has been observed for centuries and is celebrated by the town where flags are flown in the streets and bands play joyously. The parade leads to the Bristol Trader Inn where the landlord presents the traditional gift of apples to the Admiral of the Port.

West Wales Maritime Heritage Society

This Society was formed in 1984 by a group of enthusiasts, including a number of professional seafarers, service personnel and others with practical marine skills of engineering, ship-wrighting, or from the boating and yachting world. Although many members live locally others have joined from all over the UK and overseas.

The members are actively involved in the preservation of boats and maritime documents, particularly those of local interest. The library, comprises some 1200 titles and many charts of the Waterway. The fleet includes Quest, a 28ft Flamborough Coble with a dipping lugsail. Built in 1926 by Arg Hopwood this boat was a gift to the Society together with a contribution towards the cost of the substantial restoration. After years of work Quest returned afloat in 2002 since when she has become a familiar sight on the Waterway.

Quest

Undine

Undine is an 18ft motor-sailer with a gunter rig, David Williams & Sons, Aberystwyth, built her to order for David Peyton of Llanelli. Given to the Society in 1985, members restored the rig and centre plate which had been removed for fishing. The yard of Williams & Sons built all the Pembrokeshire One Designs for Pembrokeshire Yacht Club.

General Picton is a sturdy pulling boat originally built for Trinity House in 1950s as a lifeboat-cum-workboat with a dipping lugsail to "get you

General Picton

Rosyth

home". Sold into private ownership in the 1980s the next years were spent on the Waterway as a fishing boat. She was purchased for the Society by a member and after extensive repairs she is in regular use again, sailing each summer.

Rosyth is a ten foot dinghy built as a training tool for apprentice shipwrights learning their skills at Rosyth Dockyard in 1960. She became tender, first to Gasganey and then to Warden which served the SMAS for buoylifting on the West Coast.

The latest boat to join the fleet is simply known as *K3,* her fishing number, donated by Mr Ken Morgan of Llangwm she is a particular treasure as one of the last remaining compass fishing boats.

One of the aims, through using their presence at local events, is to help broaden the knowledge of maritime culture in West Wales. The Society's six craft are displayed afloat or ashore on these occasions as at their annual River Rally when the parade of traditional craft and other vessels winds its way in a spectacular procession up the Pembroke River to Castle Pool.

The Society also provides support at festivals in Neyland, Pembroke Dock and other places on the Waterway.

An interesting development has been the Society's involvement

The workshop

WWMHS at Seafair Haven in 2006

at functions in Ireland, including mounting exhibitions at Waterford Tall Ships' Festival and the New Ross 800th anniversary aboard the Dunbrody, while an ongoing link is being developed with Wexford Friends of Tall Ships. In addition the members' expertise comes into play during gatherings of tall ships and traditional boats at Seafair, Milford Haven.

Society members during Seafair 2006

Neyland Marina

Society member's vessel undergoing refurbishment at Front Street yard, Pembroke Dock.

END

© photographs: Milford Haven Port Authority, David Reed, Peter Williams, Pembrokeshire County Council, Arklow Maritime Museum, The Sunderland Trust, John Evans, David Rees. Pembrokeshire Photography